a Night
without armor

a Night without armor

*Poems*

Jewel Kilcher

 HarperEntertainment
*A Division of* HarperCollins*Publishers*

First paperback edition published 1999.

Designed by Elina D. Nudelman

The Library of Congress has catalogued the hardcover edition as
follows:

Jewel, 1974–
    A night without armor/Jewel.—1st ed.
        p. cm.
    ISBN 0-06-019198-8
    I. Title.

PS3560.E888N5    1998                               98-21593

811'.54—dc21

ISBN 0-06-107362-8 (pbk.)

    08  09              20 19 18 17

THIS BOOK IS DEDICATED TO
the One in Whom we live and move and have our being
to my parents, Nedra Carroll and Atz Kilcher
to my brothers Shane, Atz, and Nikos
and to the land which inspires my heart to sing, Alaska

# Contents

# Acknowledgments

The following have my gratitude: My grandmother
Ruth Kilcher; my family; Jacqueline Synder; my
editor, Mauro DiPreta, and my agent, Sandra Martin;
artist Pat Steir; photographer Brigitte Lacombe; Ingrid
Sischy; Bridget Hanley; Keith Anderson; BiBi Bielat;
Lee Green; and all at HarperCollins and Atlantic
Records who have worked to make this book possible.

# Preface

"Some people react physically to the magic of poetry, to the moments, that is, of authentic revelation, of the communication, the *sharing*, at its highest level. . . . A good poem is a contribution to reality. The world is never the same once a good poem has been added to it. A good poem helps to change the shape and significance of the universe, helps to extend everyone's knowledge of himself and the world around him." —Dylan Thomas (1913–1953)

From an early age, my mother would gather me and my brothers after school for "workshops" in music, visual art, and writing. I grew to love the poems of Shakespeare, Dylan Thomas, Rumi, Yeats, and others that she read to us. She read her own compositions, as well, and taught us to write our *own*. For me poetry allowed word to be given to the things that otherwise had no voice, and I discovered the strength and soul of poetry—through it we *come to know;* we are led to feel, sense, and to expand our understanding beyond words.

Long before I wrote my first song, words formed as poems in my journals; and poetry drives my song writing today. My songs are strongly influenced by Pablo Neruda, Bukowski, Octavio Paz; and musically I admire the great poetic lyricists like many of the writers of Tin Pan Alley, and others, like Bob Dylan, Joni Mitchell, Leonard Cohen, and Tom Waits. Each forged the bridge from poetry to music.

I've learned that not all poetry lends itself to music—some thoughts need to be sung only against the silence. There are softer and less tangible parts of ourselves that are so essential to openheartedness, to peace, to unfolding the vision and the spiritual realm of our lives, to exposing our souls. Poetry is a passage into those parts of our being where we understand who we have been and where we discover and decide who and what we will be. It makes us intimate with ourselves and others and with the human experience. It stirs the Divine within us and whispers all the things there are no words for, and this is essential to bring balance and dimension to the human expression.

Poetry is the most honest and immediate art form that I have found, it is raw and unfiltered. It is a vital, creative expression and deserves to find greater forums, to be more highly valued, understood, and utilized in our culture and in our lives. There is such wonderful poetry in the world that wants to be given voice. My hope is to help inspire an appreciation and expression of that voice.

# As a Child I Walked

As a child I walked
with noisy fingers
along the hemline
of so many meadows
back home

Green fabric
stretched out
  shy earth
  shock of sky

I'd sit on logs like pulpits
listen to the sermon
of sparrows
and find god in Simplicity,
there amongst the dandelion
and thorn

# The Bony Ribs of Adam

I left the bony ribs of Adam
for the fruit
of my own
personal desire

Its scent still heavy
upon my flesh
my absence still
thorn
to his side

But now how my belly
hollows and aches
   craving seed
   craving kisses
but outside the road hisses

and I find myself
packing girlishness
in an old leather bag

love stepping lightly
away from the door

# Wild Horse

I'd like to call you my wild horse
and feed you silver sage

I'd like to paint my poems
with desert tongued clay
across
your back
and ride you savagely
as the sweet and southern wind
through a green and wild Kentucky

I'd like to make you my secret sun
blazing dark and red in the orchards
and I would steal away
to watch the way
your silver belly bends
and bows beneath me

I'd make you my wings
in the foothills of Montana
my lover in the oceans of the world

I'd make you my many calico children
and scatter you
across
the green memories of home

I'd be your hungry Valley
and sow your golden fields of wheat
in my womb

## Bukowski's Widow

My prince has slipped!
and his face has turned
  to shadow

his tongue no longer strong
but gray (how sad!)
it used to be so full
  of spit and roses

My prince the stars have
fallen from your crown
And I can not fathom
their fading—
some things should be forever!

You've taken your coal
and your seaward gaze—

You've taken your will
and your weakness and left

me with nothing but
words to keep me warm
  But I don't want them!
  Take them back!

I want Paris
I want you drunk on wine
I want to walk with you
  and hold you up
and giggle and kiss

God how I miss
your smile and thick skin

At night
   (Do you remember?)
   How I'd worry
and you'd press me tight
against you. Extinguishing
   the red flame
of my head against
your shoulder
   Smooth as chalk dust you'd laugh
in the face of
death and uncertainty
   *Do you remember?*
You'd say time knew nothing
well now you're gone
   and time is all I have left

## You Tell Me

It cannot be so
    you say
simple hands
cannot change
the fate of humanity.
    I say
Humanity is
a boundless,
absorbing heart
transcending
death & generations
and centuries
absorbing bullets
and stitches
and tear gas
enduring humiliation
and illegal abortions
and thankless jobs
    I say to you
the heart of Humanity
has not
and will not
be broken
And let us raise ourselves
like lanterns
with the millions of others—
with the mad
and the forgotten
and the strong of heart
to shine

## Paramount, NY, 9:34 A.M.

In the morning tiny bells go off
that light a darkened path
Reluctant as pinpricks
dawn pierces sleep
with nimble fingers
I am unwoven
     the rich yoke of slumber
     unraveled thread by thread
until I am naked and glistening
standing before the newness
of another day
a tiny form birthed of white linen
and restless dreams

## It Has Been Long

It has been
long and
Bony since
your willing
ways since
those thirstful
days of
summer nights
and Burning Beds

## Too Many Nights

It's been
too many nights
  of being with

to now be suddenly
without

# I Look at Young Girls Now

I look at young girls now
in their tight crushed velour
skin tight sky blue
hip huggers with the baby doll
tank tops
and I think
   I've been there.
   God, have I been there.

Sixteen years old and
wrestling with an overwhelming
newfound sexuality.
Parading it in all its
raw and awkward charm.

I had a pair of vintage
burgundy velvet short-
shorts that laced up
the sides
from the 1920s
and I wore them
with a tight leotard
and a plastic faux pearl
choker

showing off all my lanky
leggy blossoming
youth on the verge
of womanhood for all the
free world to see
with no idea how to keep
a secret, especially my own.

# Seattle

Tonight on the street I saw a woman
whose hard living
had turned her into a weak man;
robbed of all softness. No magic. No awe.
She had bruised breasts and was
arguing with a drunk boyfriend
in the middle of the road.
He held her collar while her sour face
reddened and hollered and spit
until finally
he threw her down like a beetle
on its back—
her thick skin cursing.
I wanted to stare
but just kept walking like all the other passersby.
The clear bottle
of vodka in her hand
lighting up
like a watery lantern.

## Saved from Myself

How often I've cried out
in silent tongue
to be saved
from myself

in the middle of the night
too afraid
to move

horrified the answer
may be beyond the
capability of my
own two hands

so small

(no one should feel this alone)

## Taking the Slave

Burn

her eyes
without hope of
understanding them

Kiss

her mouth
that you may
fathom
its strange tongue

Indulge

in her brown skin
because
it reminds you
of Mother

Rape

her mind
because it is not your own
but so sweet
so familiar

like coming home

to a native land
your pale and inbred hands
can only faintly fathom

## Sun Bathing

I read a book
and the man thinks
I can not see
the wrinkled posture
of his son
as he is nudged.
He thinks
I can not sense
four eyes
upon my flesh
as the father tries
to bond with
his teenage boy
by ogling my breasts.

## Red Roof Inn, Boston

I miss you miserably, dear
and I can't quite manage
to face this unbearably
large bed
alone.

I find myself avoiding sleep

busying myself with
menial chores

so I pick up my guitar

stare at books with bleary eyes

get restless then shave
my armpits with your razor
and cheap hotel soap.

## So Just Kiss Me

So just kiss me and let my hair
messy itself in your fingers

tell me nothing needs to be done—
no clocks need winding

There is no bell without a voice
needing to borrow my own

instead, let me steady myself
in the arms

of a man who won't ask me to be
what he needs, but lets me exist

as I am

    a blonde flame
    a hurricane

wrapped up
in a tiny body

that will come to his arms
like the safest harbor

    for mending

## Second Thoughts in Columbus, Ohio

I find it strange that we search
our whole lives for love
as though it were the
final treasure
the solemn purpose of people
in movies and magazines.
Yet when it comes to your door
one morning with calm eyes to deliver itself
you realize it alone is not enough.

You are before me, sweet man,
and I am thinking
Aren't I supposed to give up
everything?
Aren't I supposed to be brave
and abandon
each dream and aspiration
and yield utterly to this
elusive beast love,
to your soft belly and companionship?

Aren't we supposed to
have a piece of land—and children!—
that look like you, and cook
soup and bread and sing
each other songs before sleep
and absentmindedly count the stars
from our front porch as we pray
for each other's keep
and pretend
forever is a word known
not only by the heart?

# Cautious

You don't call

    anymore.
You say
it hurts
    too much
your heart
like one of
those
    fragile cactus flowers
cast amongst
thorny ribs.

So ready
to be
hurt.

# The Dark Bells

The dark bells
of midnight
tolled
for no others—
those were our names
rising forth
from their rusty throats
like small birds
falling from the nest.

My heart turned seaward,
sea-sick from
all the things
I would have to tell you . . .
My hands
pale knives
that held your face
in the twilight
of our bedroom,
in the turbulence
of our hearts.
My tongue
    (the same tongue
    that kissed you!)
endeavored, with
tiny incisions, successful as paper cuts,
to free you
from my side.
The dark weight of the hour
humming madly

filling my head
with blood
and sorrow
and dread
the executioner's song.

## The Inertia of a Lonely Heart

The world is full of cripples
and endless nights
and broken fruit
and calls that never come through
and restless dreams
   that fear being awake
and stars that lose themselves
and waves that are always leaving
and bitten mouths
and lonely bars
and rosy nipples
   rosy as dawn
   rosy as the first blush of youth
and tired people
and lonely hearts
opening, orbiting
crashing into open mouths
and hungry eyes
and empty-handed lovers;
the inertia of loneliness
a miserable force

## Collect Beads of Night

Collect beads of night
Fill your
skin with the dark weight of the
wet sky. Let boldness live in your heart
and I will recognize you
amongst the many
and claim you
as my own

# Communion

my flesh melts
on your tongue

my breast dissolves
beneath your desire

my ears turn to wind;

roots reclaim my veins.

My stomach disappears
with its lunar twin

water taking my will until

I am reduced to a glimmer

boiled down to a spark

sifted into tiny stone

that has many wings
nesting inside your palm

# Love Poem

We made love last night
beneath the stars.
The moon's Cycloptic eye
unblinking
staring us down
uncovering our bodies of the darkness
like naked roots
we tangled ourselves
thighs and elbows heavy fruit
shiny as winter chestnuts.
Body of the man I love—
bitten mouth, tangerine lips
rose petal surprise of tongue,
I could wander the continent
of your golden valleys
without ceasing
and delight each day
in discovering
a new dawn
rising from the depths
of your mysterious being.

# Father of a Deaf Girl

Every time her hands began to stutter he became
enraged. She threw these fits sometimes, and he
never took the time to understand what they meant.
Her words were wasted on him. Her hands useless
birds caged by their quietness, and he would
immobilize them, tying her wrists together so they'd
jump like awkward fish, gasping at the shock of air.
Un-heard they'd dance like that for hours, her eyes
full of silent desperation, on the other side of the
closet door. He never even knew what they were
saying.

> *I want to fly from here! I want to fly from*
> *here! I want to fly from here! I want to fly*
> *from here! I want to fly from here! I want*
> *to fly from here!*

# Dionne & I

We looked in the fridge only to see moldy Kraft singles and some eye cream. That eye cream was our pride and joy, so extravagant and luxurious, it made us feel rich. The cracked walls of the bathroom fading away into the small lights of her tiny vanity mirror.

We may have had no food, but we knew the eye cream was all we needed—we were both young, with pretty faces and a lot of faith in the system.

 Some men would take us out.

# 1B

The woman sitting next to me
in 1B has burn marks on her hands.
As she sleeps, I let myself stare
trying to figure out
if it was a cooking accident
or . . .

She boarded quietly,
but her eyes
grazed me with
malignant anger.

She is awake now.
I turn away,
look out the window.
Reaching for the phone
the sleeve of her business jacket lifts, revealing
a neat row of round burn marks
all up her forearm.

Was she hurt as a child?
Was it a late husband,
mean boyfriend, crazy sex fetish?

I try to catch the title
of the book she's reading
for clues.

It's just some mystery novel.

I can tell
I'm making her
uneasy.
I go back to my writing.

She looks so hard—
like a lot of women in L.A.
Dark secrets hunting her insides,
softness sucked out,
a deep sadness in her eyes.

# The Slow Migration of Glaciers

The slow migration of glaciers
unfolding through the centuries
their heavy wing
burdened with all the
weight of the earth
they move and carve and breathe

swollen rivers thick with soot
my pony and I drawing
    deep sharp breaths
as we cross
submerged
in all that is natural and Holy

To run free with you once more
to let my hair tangle itself
in a wind that knows only motion

to lose my heart once again
in the thorns of primrose
on the plains of Fox River Valley
lost in a maze of Timothy and Blue Grass hay.

These are the things which made me
these are the things I call home
these are the things that have filled
my heart with song and I raise them now in homage:

my father and I riding until after dark
chasing cattle or startling eagles into flight
cooking on a coal stove

cutting meat with a dull knife
my hands raw from picking rose hips
on the sea cliffs above Kackamack Bay
staring endlessly at the blue sky . . .

Few would guess now how much I miss
you Alaska

how my heart grows
heavy out here

so far away

So much talk
so much noise
strangling all stillness
so I can no longer
hear the voice of god whisper
to me in the silence

I will return to you, Alaska,
my beloved, but for now
I am youth's soldier
chasing down
an endless dawn

# Tai Pei

Midnight.
Blackest sky
Outside my window I can see
A stranger's tongue
wagging and winding its way
through its native streets.

But this is not my home.

I am the stranger here,
with no language but my pen.

Sex fills the air.
It is humid and ancient.
Many lovers have been taken down
exalted, fallen, risen
kissed by the purple finger
that seeks the plum blossomed Love.

I have no Lover
only my pen and an
answering machine
back in the States which
no one calls.

I am told
I am adored by millions
but no one calls.

# Tai Pei 2

Thick night, a cobalt expanse
littered with the bright shock
of yellow and orange neon signs
boasting their wares,
dried fruit or wedding dresses
in the latest style.

A humid claw clings to me,
every movement anticipated
by this moist air,
this Asian sky
with its endless fields
yawning unseen beneath it.

Somewhere out there, an overhead fan
is spinning, ticking, rattling.
A young girl sweats, her
armpits like tidy rosebuds.
The businessman
from Hong Kong pretends to have
fallen asleep while
she washes herself in the sink,
the night sticking to her
insides in a way she can't wash off.

# Tai Pei 3

A warm rain swept across
the streets. Filling spaces
with humid quiet. White noise.
Moist gauze
dulling the edge of
the vendors' pleas.

Woman selling incense
outside the temple. Huge bronze bowls
bellowing smoke,
the room
thick with choking fragrance.

Women of prayer with deep lines
in their faces and blue robes
blessing those who come to them
seeking clarity.

The click-clack of wax pieces
as they are dropped upon the
stone floors, wet with rain,
by a devotee to see if his
prayers have been answered.

The warm mellow golden hue
of the red ceremonial candles
lit in interlocking circles that
climb, circle upon circle, into
a darkening sky.
Fog and rain hanging low and heavy
like a damp and woolen hood.

On the steps below there is a man
with one leg, whose face
looks carved of wood
    a hysteric smile
      parting his lips.
He reads people's palms.

## In the South of England Somewhere

In the south of England somewhere
they race lawn mowers
The fastest goes 65 miles an hour
at top speed
with no head wind

I don't know how men run along behind them
Unless it's the kind you sit on—
which seems like cheating

There is a museum there
run by a fanatic
He has memorized and catalogued
the sound each mower makes
noting fondly his favorite three

There are also worm charming contests
Three people to a team
One to charm
one to collect
one to count

Local John McCallister reassures us,
"It's on a strictly catch and release basis, of course."

# 1966

I turned off the TV.
Looked out of my window
to the streets below.
Dry sidewalks.
A line had straightened up
stiff as uncut ribbon
beneath a sign
that read Army Headquarters.

I stared at the boys' faces.
They looked itchy and awkward
like my brother's. I don't know
what kept them in that line,
the sun was hot and unrelenting.

I wondered if my brother
would stand in line, too.
I wondered if it would take him somewhere.
I wondered if all the brothers
in all the world were leaving,
and if there would only be us sisters left
to occupy the empty rooms
with doll clothing and postcards.

## A Couple Sitting on a Bench

He's the skinny one of the two.
He reminds her of it constantly.
He's a very funny guy that way—
ha-ha as she wobbles-to-walk wobbles-to-walk.

# Envy

passionless bodies
with pointless little limbs
that flaunt in vain
such narrowness of frame
with nothing to offer but bone

# Pretty

There is a pretty girl
on the
Face
of the magazine
And
all I can see
are my dirty
hands
turning the page

## Those Certain Girls

I am fascinated by
those certain girls
    you know the ones
the women that are always girls
their tiny bodies like
neglected willow trees
    controlled and contorted
which may blow away with
the slightest disappointment

## Sausages

While leaving the airport,
a gypsy woman stole my luggage.
She wore a rice paper mask over her eyes.
A mole showed neatly on her chin,
hairless. She laughed while sausages
fell from her pockets in heavy shivers.
I hope she misses them sorely.

# Though I am 8

Though I am 8, my father is 63 years old.
He drinks concoctions of chickweed, garlic, and ordinary
grass
pulled out of the front lawn. He blends it with
a machine that wakes me every morning.
It makes a loud growl. He is worried, I think,
he won't make it to my high school graduation.

Outside, winter swallows my footsteps
as quickly as they are laid,
which makes me cry.

# Dylan

I had a dream last night
that a little girl came to me.
Her hair was a halo of warm light
and color dripped off her tongue

She was your daughter
and in her I saw the fruit
of everything I'd ever fought for
or believed in, or dreamt of.

# Vincent Said

Vincent said she was like screwing a corpse,
but a 16-year-old corpse with young tits,
so it wasn't bad. She left the door open
while he pretended to be asleep
and did the walk o' shame
through the hotel lobby.

I know his girlfriend, Phyllis,
but I won't tell her.
It's not for me to judge
or discriminate just because
she does
and he won't.

# Camouflage

A gay man
is sitting in
a hotel lobby
    smoking
a cigarette.
He stomachs my
breasts dutifully
like spinach or lima beans
or other things that
make one sick
because he fears
the red-necks
    at the bar
are on to him.

## Sara Said

i used to screw without condoms
and let the man
come inside me because
i was too shy
to stop him

then i'd go home
and pray on my pillow
please
please
please
don't let me get pregnant

i couldn't sleep
or eat
  just think

of my 15-year-old life
with a child
PLEASE GOD
DON'T LET ME
GET PREGNANT

then i would bleed
and find relief
until i was at last
at another man's mercy

an open vessel
whose function it was
to be filled
until my consciousness
could return and
spit out
the bad seeds

## Parking Lot

It was the way
my thigh felt against
the cool car hood
that made me
like you so

And it was the way
a risk can run down
a spine that made
my blood race
as a few bleary eyes
stumbled to their cars
unaware

And it was the way
you took me with such
strength and stretched
me between the
moon and a Chevrolet
that made me
crave you so

## Coffee Shop

Young girls wrap themselves tightly
in bright smiles and denim,

no more patent leather
and pigtails here.

They suck on coffee,
with great indifference,
their young thighs
weapons they have cocked,
hardly comprehending
the potency which lies
in suggestion.

Tight, dark, dark blue
wrangler jeans
and lonely smiles like
latent prophecies.

## I Say to You Idols

I say to you idols
of carefully studied
disillusionment

And you worshipers
who find beauty
in only fallen things

that the greatest
Grace
we can aspire to
is the strength
to see the wounded
walk with the forgotten
and pull ourselves
from the screaming
blood of our losses
to fight on
undaunted
all the more

## Steady Yourself

Steady yourself, love,
steady yourself
for victory is near
Shut out the world
with its tyranny
of noise
     none of this matters now
Draw strength from
the vision the deepest
folds of your soul
so longs for
For it is a song we all sing
Steady yourself, love,
upon my gaze
in this corridor
& waver not in the face
of the battle cry

We will not be beaten!
Lose not your faith now
for I need it to strengthen my own
and should your steps
falter, mine would
grow lonely in this
world of coal and roses

We are the living
and the living
must love the world
It is our duty
to fill our hearts

with all the anguish and joy
of our brothers and sisters
Steady yourself, love,
be strong beside me
and know that our
unrelenting gives them
dis-ease, and that
the clearer your mouth
raises itself in
songs of freedom
the more others will come to
warm themselves around
the flag of your faith
For our numbers grow
and soon will outweigh
their tattered armies
and I want your heart
to rejoice in its
inevitable victory

## Awaken, Love

Awaken love,
the sun beats itself
upon our windowsill
and dawn is well spent into day
Awaken, love
open your eyes
lighting all they touch upon
in wondrous blaze

Upon the streets
a kitten's mew
and beggar's shoe
are calling
and the voiceless
ask to borrow yours
so sweet and
always falling

Awaken love,
we are a pair
two knives, two flags
two slender stocks of wheat
And the song that sleeps
inside your mouth
is the song which bids
my heart to beat

For without your hands
your battle cry
your timid fearless
roaming eye

I would be awkward hands
with no flag
with no pulse
no boast to brag

but alone, simply
Alone

Staring down
an endless sky
unable to face
injustice
or even I
A tiger's loveless soldier

# Gather Yourself

Gather yourself at the seashore
and I will love you there

Assemble yourself with wild things
with songs of the sparrow and sea foam

Let mad beauty collect itself
in your eyes and it will shine, calling me

For I long for a man
with nests of wild things in his hair

A man who will kiss the flame

# You

You with your
    gentle lightning
spinning like Orion,
    full of muscle
and all the patience
    of stars.
Hooked upon the pinnacle
    of a desire
that arrests
    itself,
caught on the crosswires
    of what could be,
my mind turns to you:
    A pin hole of light
    that softly hums
    and murmurs
whose blurry edges
    beg to come into view.

## Bleary eyed

Bleary eyed
    and sleepy still
I unwrapped you
    of the morning
like careful fruit
    with forbidden flesh
made sweeter by
    the scorning

My hands still shaky
    from kisses sweet
and the dark hours
    of night's embrace
I checked to see
    if fastened vines
my heart had left
    in silv'ry trace

While you slept
    I looked inside your chest
to see what there
    was growing
I saw my heart
    with quiet eyes
to your side its self
    was gently sewing

I saw my heart
    with quiet eyes
to your side its self
    was gently sewing

# I Miss Your Touch

I miss your touch
    all taciturn
like the slow migration of birds
nesting momentarily
upon my breast
    then lifting
silver and quick—
sabotaging the landscape
with their absence

my skin silent without
      their song
a thirsty pool of patient flesh

# Night Falls

Night falls
    and keeps on
falling
    Autumn leaves
bruise the sky
    a yellow shiver
ripping the smooth hour
    with its edgy
spine
    Struggling to hold back
the dawn
    open-hearted lovers
cling to the sweet fruits
    of last-minute kisses
so eager
    to lose themselves
in the honey-thick gravity
    of love so new
while beyond the Gates
    leaves tear themselves
from the only limb they've known
    to experience
the freedom
    the uncertainty
of air

## We Have Been Called

We have been called
    naive
as if it were
a dirty word
We have been called
    innocent
as though with shame
our cheeks should burn
So
We visited with
the careful idols
of cynicism
to learn to sneer
and pant and walk
    so as not to feel the scales
    of judgment rub wrongly
But we say
    some things must
    remain simple
    some things must remain
    untouched
    and pure
lest we all forget
the legacy which begot us
the health of our origins
the poetry of our fundamental selves

And so
it is to
the longing hearts we sing

rise! spread
your wings!
Let no hand
nor ill will
keep you.

# Underage

I hung out once in the bathroom of Trade Winds Harley
    bar in Anchorage
with several biker chicks for company until the cops left.
They had pale skin and thick black eye makeup
and they asked me to sing at their weddings.
I said I'd ask my dad.

We all sat on the counter and waited for the pigs to leave.
Some guy O.D.'d and was outside foaming at the mouth.

I remember looking in the mirror
and seeing this white face,
my shirt all buttoned up.
The women were nice to me
and looked like dark angels
beside me. I liked them,
and together we waited
patiently for the cops to leave,
so I could go back out
and join my dad up
on stage.

# Grimshaw

Grimshaw came to T's Homestead
each time Dad and I played a gig,
which was every Tuesday night.
Behind his round spectacles,
his eyes looked sad and small as whales'-eyes.
His beard was wild and full of birds nests, I supposed.

He had a routine I knew well:
He'd organize his money in neat stacks
and let me choose any bill I wanted
(I took two 1's for Shirley Temples),
And request 3 songs:
Ain't Goin' to Study War No More,
House of the Rising Sun,
Green Green Fields of Home.
Then order four pitchers of beer,
which he lined up on his corner table.
Grimshaw was quiet and didn't scare me.
He always said please to Sally the waitress.

One Tuesday he didn't show up.
The next week, we asked Sally and she told us
Grimshaw had shot himself in the face.

Sally said that all of us at the bar
were the closest thing to a family he had,
and so Dad and I sang on a Saturday afternoon
in the gravel parking lot to raise money
for a proper funeral.

I came up to everyone's belt buckle
and had to crank my neck back
to look up at all the adults.
So I just studied people's waistlines and listened
to the disjointed melody of the broken men
gathered into a loose knot for the tavern wake.
One man's face was worn out but his eyes were bright.
He said, "He has a cabin out on Fox Road."
Another winked down at me saying,
"I sure hope he's happy."
They all talked about him as if he were still alive.

I found out Grimshaw went to Nam when he was 18,
to be a surgeon when he wasn't one.
He had to hurt people until he learned.

I stood that day among the bar flies and regulars
and made a vow—the kind a child makes—
to face things as they came
so they wouldn't compound with time and become
like huge ships, impossible to turn around.

# A Slow Disease

My dad went to Vietnam when he was 19 years old.
I think it bruised his soul. There are some things
the human mind should never have to comprehend, some
    things the body never can forget
He doesn't talk about it. Actually, I guess, I've never
    asked,
I hate to imagine his puppy young eyes absorbing all that
    rain and mud and blood.
The jungles must have seemed like a slow disease
that would continue to
arrest his and so many other hearts
the rest of their lives.

# All the Words

All the words I wish your fingers could feel

all the times I've wished
you could know
the silent sorrow
   lying stiff in my throat
like cold
and broken teeth

I wish you could hear
the child that cries
in my flesh and makes
my bones ache

*I wish you could speak to my fear*

I wish you could hold me
in your arms like oceans
and soothe what my muscles remember
   all the bruises, all the sour hope
   all the screams and scraped knees
the cloudy days so dark
I wondered if my eyes
were even open

The days that I felt
like August, and that I, too
would soon turn
to Fall

# You Are Not

you are not
the brave soldier

Neruda's sons
Chaves' brother

you are not
the dark horse
heart filled
with all the weight
and compassion
your hardships
have won you
you are not
driven by the need
to free all people
from meanness and
loveless abuse
    I know you
you are asleep in your church
on Sunday afternoon
looking for god
in answers you seek
through others
instead
of being the answers
you are praying for peace
but unwilling to be it

praying for mercy
but unwilling to give it

praying for Love
but too busy
making sure you got your own:
  a good job
  a good girl
all the trimmings you are
entitled to
all the bells and whistles
that are meaningful
but only to those who possess
a heart most common

## The Strip 1

Here I am
on the strip.
The Main attraction.
My name up
in lights.
What's there to do, pussy cat?
  (Nothingnotmuchverylittle.)
My hair is clean
it's the night before
the show.
New Year's Eve.
Downstairs
young people are being young,
gambling, kissing.
I'm in my room eating licorice,
looking at myself
in the mirror,
the flower of youth
sighing and blooming
for hotel art
and stale walls.
What's the news, jack?
  (Nothingnotmuchverylittle.)

# The Strip 2

no one slept last night
not hardly
in Las Vegas

what a way to rush in
the new year
Start it off right, right?

I left my hotel
    at 3 A.M.
crossed the street
to buy water
there was a dead body
in the middle of the road
no one had seen it yet
I suppose
but me

# Shush

Can you imagine
how silent
a plane crash would be
if you were deaf?

How unbearably loud a rape?

## I Am Not from Here

I am not from here,
my hair smells of the wind
and is full of constellations
and I move about this world
with a healthy disbelief
and approach my days and my work
with vaporous consequence
   a touch that is translucent
   but can violate stone.

# Infatuation

infatuation is a strange thing
a bony creature thin
with feeding on itself

it is addicted not to its subject
but to its own vain hunger
and needs but a pretty face
to fuel its rampant imagination
   humid couch
    and sweaty palms
    fleshy carpets
    ablaze with conquest
but when conquering is complete
the blood leaves its limbs
and it becomes disenchanted
(to the point of disgust)
with its subject
who sits then like a hollow trunk
emptied of its precious cargo
and left to fade
   a seed relieved
of its transparent husk
to dissolve, finally
on a rough
and impatient
tongue

# The Fall

Labor to open
the large wooden door
wrestle the wind
as it sucks past
and rushes through the house
greedily.

Step into the crisp day
blue sky, dry leaves
   shocked to see
the sun still shining.

It had grown so dark in there

Breathe in deeply,
the thin air
flashing lungs that have been
crying
tied in knots talking to you again again again

We try too hard—
Do you see?

# Long Has a Cloak

Long has a cloak of coarse wool
and wet feathers smothered my flight.
Long has doubt and a thorny chain of words
caused my vision to stagger.
Tired of my purple burden,
in search of freedom, I have longed to throw
off the gauze curtains and kisses
which bind me
    my mouth so full of berries
    and other people's tongues
my heart sick with thick hands and spittle.
*But there is a secret I do not tell you;*
    I have dulled my spark
    and weakened my heart
    so I could continue
    to stay where I knew
    I did not flourish
      (There. It is said.)
To stand new in the naked air
with no crutch, no pretty eye,
I leave not only you
but also the part of me
that fears my own song's truth.

# Mercy

I'm leaving

You're done

Cut the cord

I will bare my heart

Make sure it's sharp

Make it quick

Flash your will against me
relieve this red smear
Smother the beating
dull the pulse
Show mercy
Spare it from your side
and I will rip
what was yours, what was living in me,
and return it to you.

Do it while our hearts
are still intact
before they rot in each other's care
before they become riddled with bitterness
choked by the stinking seeds
of resentment.

# Compass

Together we have sensed distance
stretch its defeating spine
between our hearts, and felt the
haunted gales of vacancy fill
the hollows of our eyes with wandering.

There is no thief to blame who has
stolen the warmth from
our kisses; departure has been gradual,
by degrees.
          Because I love you
I will not send you into the night
with teeth marks and pride I have
stripped you of.  I will draw
a compass on your belly, and you
will tell my heart that it's okay
before we turn each other loose beneath
the endless sky. Let us be still.
          Tell the arms not to worry so.
          Disarm the tongue of its dagger
                    and listen.

Such cold beauty exists here
*Do you see it?*  Like the landscape,
frozen, waiting to be born.

# Freedom

Having mutilated
and freed myself
from the very wings
which for so long
held me aloft
I have cast my heart
like a purpled fruit
toward the violent earth,
far from the Heaven
of your arms

# Road Spent

I could stand to be alone
for some time
Lose myself in white noise
slip into the blur
contemplate the color yellow
    Right now
I just don't handle splashes too well
Or too many teeth
around me all at once
armed like guns with something to say
Urgent whispers
hoarse restraint
    Quiet as paper cuts
people steal me away
cart my flesh off in tiny crimson piles
my bones have been sore
Rattling against each other
in their anemic cage
ravens circling
my heart beating
it's-time  to-go  it's-time  to-go
someplace full of surf
full of flat blue sky
full of shuuushhh

# Christmas in Hawaii

The sky pierces me
with its turquoise embrace.
The scent of lemons
and suntan oil find
their way to me
by the pool:
No one is here.
I walk the beaches alone
and drink silly concoctions
with little paper umbrellas.
In my room, my guitar
is calling to me.
I will go to it soon
and write songs
for love lost
and for love yet to come.
Merry Christmas, baby,
  goodnight.

## Spoiled

I am perhaps
unfaithful
to those who
are outside my
own flesh.

I can not help
it, I am an
opportunist—
each pretty
face should
come with a straw
so that I may
slurp up the
perfect moments
without them getting
stuck between
my teeth.

# Red Light District, Amsterdam

Silver threads, a delicious mark
steel kiss ignites a spark
not just once, but maybe twice
I don't wanna write sad songs tonight

Under a strong moon my heart swells up
I'm overflowing, Buttercup.
Give me a strong arm not weak with might
don't wanna sing sad songs tonight

Daffodils and daisies hot on my chest
sweet arms, salty flesh.
Sweet and proud I'm sharp as a dart,
do you wanna see a blue bird? It sings in the dark.

Not just once but maybe twice
I don't wanna sing no sad songs tonight

## Lovers for Lilly

Boys with faces like
calm puddles
begging to be
messied up

    stirred
    aroused

deliver themselves
to her doorstep

    messy hair
    morning mouth

She welcomes them in
entertains their curiosity
with the dry well,
the empty wealth
of her years

Lovers for Lilly

she eats them
like fruit cake

Lovers for Lilly

she collects them
like flies

Lovers for Lilly

(are always good-byes).

## Lemonade

Moths beat themselves
upon the screen door
of some other afternoon

A red dress burns in my mind

Outside the hound is turning
a lantern over that had
been left out in the rain

I long for a hot day
when moist palms reach
for my warmth and pull
me down to some humid
and reckless depth

Night spilling over me
its velvet stain

# We Talk

We talk
    slowly
about nothing
about movies
    we stick to
surface streets
    and find no
meaning in café windows
no substance in
    hotel rooms
I used to unwrap you!
tender layers unfolding
like eager gold
    but now
we are cool
and recount
our daily bores
    as though
the sum of our
    uses
equaled
    something
    (more)
substantial
    while softer
things shrivel
    and dry roots

go unfed
        strangled
by the phone line
and all
        that is
        not said

## Spivey Leaks

Spivey Leaks was a drip of a man.
He looked like a potato shoved into jeans.
He was 45 and loved Jesus so much
it made him hyperventilate
when the kids would tease him on it,
on their ways home from school.
He wanted to squash them all like gnats,
and would have, too—which
is a good argument for perpetuating
the threat of Hell, I suppose.

## Forgetful

he walks with a skin of stone
in effort to keep his blood
from dirtying the pavement

he closes his eyes
with deliberate determination
trying to remember

the veins behind his eyes
lead like blue road maps
to the ocean of everyone else

# Lost

Lost
is a puzzle
of stars
that breathes
like water
and chews
like stone

Alone
is a reminder
of how far
acceptance
is from
understanding

Fear
is a bird
that believes itself
into extinction

Desperation
the honest recognition
of a false truth

Hope
seeing who you really are
at your highest
is who you will become

Grace
the refinement of a
Soul through time

## Still Life

Orange
tired eye
dry upon the table
constant longing
  in love with the sun

Dawn
fiery arms
that wish only
to embrace a sea
too big to be held

Bones
why do I even try?
A constant ache
a constant dry thirst
a scratch beneath
  a sheet of steel

Non-vision
a strange hour
neither awake nor dead
just asleep
in a room
that dreams itself
  into being

Conspiracy
a million watery ears
beneath our skin to hear
that we all want to be each other
  (that we already are)

# I Don't Suppose Raindrops

I don't suppose raindrops
will ever replace
the sound of small feet

nor sunflowers
their tiny crowns

All the dust has gathered itself
and settled on
   your heart
and there is no correct combination

no key

no question

that will deliver them
once more
to your side

for she has already decided:
   *no answers will*
   *be given*

## Sometimes

Sometimes
I feel
my heart
fall
to vague depths
between
words there
are such
spaces that
I can't help
but feel
My Heart
fall
between
the pregnant pause
of all you will
not say
and all
I can
not ask

# Blanketed by a Citrus Smile

blanketed by a citrus smile
your splash of sincerity evades me
your aim not at fault
I just have no faith left
for it to stick to

it is strange how in just
a few short months
I can look back on myself
like a stranger
    and you
(whom I loved?!)
      are like cumulous clouds
dull day after day
with your threats of thunder
and promises of passion

I await the blue flame!
doused in nutmeg!
wrapped in white linen!

but as you pass over me
there is no torrid sea
no humid embrace

just pools cooling
in the small of my back

I stare at my hands
and wonder
how they got
so far away

# The Road

I have just
        caught a glimpse
of what my life
is to become
for a second I could see
        around the curve
and wondered where you were
your bright face
        no longer
beside the road
your hands
        no longer lending
themselves to familiarity

I saw Love
in the rear view mirror
with its red skirt
about its knees
        trying
to catch up
and before the curve
swallowed itself again
I remember
        thinking
There is all this love
but nowhere for it to grow
each second continually
devours the next
and we're moving too fast
for it to fasten
its roots
to the wind

# I Guess What I Wanted Was

I guess what I
wanted was
to hear

you'd stay with me always.

I guess what I
wanted was
to see

those hands vowing
never to leave my own.

I guess what
I wanted was
to know

I am not loving in vain.

# Insecurity

you don't call
I check again
I become uneasy—
   is this a frame?
Suddenly I'm not so sure
I check my sources
each conversation becomes a crumb
how easily I'm led
how stupid I've been
to believe
you could be
loving me
you who can not be seduced
by anything other than
the temperance
of need
   each one facilitating the next
and suddenly I see my place
the phone rings
you say hello
but I don't believe you

## I Am Patient

I am patient
but do not push

for it is silently
my heart will break
one night
   and with no words
you will find me gone
come morning

# The Things You Fear

The things you fear
                    are undefeatable
not by their nature
                    but by your approach

# The Chase

And now it begins
you will see.
Once you are gone
my game gets stronger.
In love with the pursuit
I will seduce you,
with ink,
blot out the night
and invent new stars.
I will sew you to my side
nevermore shall you roam
without the outline of my chase
branded on your heart.

# Fragile

Fine. If that's the way you want it.
I will walk away with all the finality
and coldness you accuse me of, but
it won't be what you expect—
a retaliation, a scene, a tangle.
It will be your jaw
flapping like an archaic flag
limp with contemplation.

# I'm Writing to Tell You

I'm writing
this letter to tell you

I don't love you anymore.

I don't miss you.

I never have.

The truth is, I
tried, but never found
your adoration
anything other than arduous,

your niceties clichéd,

your praise thoughtless,

and it has become
unbearably obvious
that you love me with
all the originality
of romance novels;

the manly man weakening
the luscious flower.

But do not be sad,
nothing is lost,
neither of us even loved
the other truly—
you only thought you did
and I only wanted to.

## And So to Receive You

And so to receive you
*to receive you*
with the tenderness of flight,
an orange blossom
caught in my throat.
The cat is purring softly
in the cobalt blue of night,
such a sweet whisper
lodged in my chest.
I hold your head
    with both hands.
Barns are burning
    somewhere out there
  (in here).
My grandmother had pale hands
that looked like sturdy veins.
She wrote poetry, too, and sang.
Though she knew few lovers,
I hope her breasts were admired
as mine are
    two silver deities
    two shining steeples
    giving testament to the sky.

My breasts are twin moons
two pillows
for your whiskered cheek
a harbor for your teeth
    and tongue.

Oh, infinite embrace!
The night has a chill
and I feel
I could not get you
close enough.

# Fat

there she sat,
a mound of flesh
with just two eyes
to comprehend the
extensiveness of
her being

she made a mountain
of herself
so no one could look down,

so no one would miss
or fail to see
the tiny woman hands
that talked desperately
of delicate things
through a fist full of rings
to all who would
stop
and listen.

# Junky

mamma says she knows what
i'm gonna grow up to be

## Austin, TX, Sheraton Hotel, 2 A.M.

His empty Vodka tonics stand
like rotted tree trunks
emptied of their core

They are on the table
where my altar rests
sharing space with my sacred things
    my rocks and reminders of home

Should I fear you?

# I Keep Expecting You To

I keep expecting you
      to fade
to wake up one morning
and not care
so I
keep myself
one carefully measured step away
      in anticipation
of your love's decline

so when your cheek turns
and your attention
      wanders
elsewhere
my heart will not be left
all awkward
      hanging
from an elastic thread
you forgot to pull off
your old pair of socks

for it's in your nature to
lose interest suddenly
      we are both artists
      who suck the marrow out
      of each lovely bone

It just happens to be
my lovely bones
this time

How Bare

# P.S.

I wrote you those nice
poems only because
the honest ones
would frighten you

# Gold Fish

In my belly is a gold fish.
I swallowed it and kept it there.
I sing to it, and can feel it wiggle
when it especially likes the tune—
Brahms makes it do backflips of glee.

# New Moon

I am in love
with a man
who is gone now
hunting
for vision
His bones
know the
scent of it
His hands full of
intuition
and praise
What he lacks
he seeks
And I watch him
from my hill
As he treads
the countryside
and splits the great
and fertile valleys
like the hips of
a woman
he has loved
for centuries
in many forms

As an eagle
a warrior
a stone

I love him

Over there

Far from me

## Someone to Know Me

At first it seemed shocking
but now the idea
tickles my tongue.
and intrigues my curiosity
beyond the ability
to rationalize or resist:

I want to live with you!

I want to wake
each morning
in your arms

comforted by your oddness

seduced by your knowledge
of my ways.

I want to care for you

brush your hair
put lotion on your scars

and pet you at bedtime,
watching your eyes close slow
   like a child's
heavy with the thousand things
that filled your day.

# Traffic

Throw yourself
into the traffic of
his desire
   unpredictable
   red sports car
no helmet in hand
your heart a potential
red smear
in the hindsight of
his rear view mirror

# Home

Harsh winter falls
away with swollen berries.
My winter-worn tongue gray
with waiting,
dull with no color all
winter long.
Small deep-red watermelon berries
full of blue sky
and all the unfathomable
flavor of spring,
tart green gooseberries and
peach-colored cloud berries
in the fall,
wild blueberries on my chin,
the blush of cranberries high in their bushes.

Stop alongside
the canyon's edge,
lose my fingers in the tangles
of the wild strawberry patch,
my hands deep in
thorny rose hips and raspberries.
Knots of swollen berries
sticking to my stained palms.

August spent
filling empty milk cartons,
canning and preserving
the syrups, jams and jellies
that would sustain us
through another pale December.

## After the Divorce

After the divorce
we moved to Homer
to live in a one bedroom apartment
behind Uncle Otto's machine shop.

My brothers slept in the water closet
after my dad painted it any color
they wanted. The pipes looked like
silver trees sprouting up through
the frames of their bunk beds.

For me, we took the door
off the coat closet
and built a narrow bed
four feet off the ground
with a ladder of rough wood
to climb up that hurt my bare feet.
My dad tried hard
to keep us all together
and work at the same time,
but things just weren't the same.
He pulled my hair when he brushed it
and didn't sing to us at night
befor we went to sleep.

I was eight and started cooking.
Shane grocery shopped
and Atz, well, he was a kid.
By 7 A.M. every morning
we walked ourselves out to the road

and waited for the school bus
with all the other kids.
Looking for signs
of when life might strike random again
and scatter us like seeds
on the unknowable winds
of chance.

# May Brought Longer Days

### I

May brought longer days and better chores.
No more throwing hay to the livestock
in sub-zero temperatures, no more waking early
to light a fire, and no more school.

Instead the days were filled with summer work,
good sweaty work: branding cattle, breaking horses,
mending fences that fell in winter.
Long days were spent cutting hay
and raking it into neat rows
to be baled and then hauled into the barn.
Working on my tan, covered in cooking oil,
driving our old tractor, Alice, my eyes would search the
    horizon,
soaking in the ease
of outdoors; of summer and its particular toil.

### II

Summer's passing was told in salmon runs,
our subsistence nets on the beach fat with their slippery
    bodies.
Weeks spent bleeding birch trees to make
syrup, canning vegetables
and drying fish in
the smoke house.

Soon the bustle of August rushed us back into our houses
where we again became confined to the logs, the coal,
and the barrel stove for another long season.

## Crazy Cow

Shane came back in from evening feed
and said, "Crazy Cow is missing."
Dad finished whatever he was eating
and casually said,
"She is probably calving."

We all knew the odds of
finding the cow in 80 acres
of wooded pasture at night were slim
but still we pulled on our
boots and coats and
headed out with flashlights
into the frozen night.
It was Shane, I think,
who found the calf tangled up in a snow bank,
half alive.
Dad picked it up in one swoop
and looked over his shoulder at the cow.
"Stupid cow," he said.
"Stupid cow," the three of us chimed,
trying not to act amazed.

On the way back to the cabin
the calf quit breathing.
We ran the rest of the way
to the front porch,
the cold air
piercing my lungs and freezing
the little hairs in my nostrils.

Orders were given:
build up the fire,
rub the calve's limbs,
get the blood going.

On the rough wood floor
of that one room cabin
I watched Dad
lean down and wrap his mouth
around the calf's tiny pink nose
fill its lungs,
and then repeat.

His big hands
handled the tiny animal expertly;
the same hands I feared
now seemed more powerful
and merciful than god's.

The Chinese lantern above us
threw a warm glow across the room.
The calf came to, coughing and spitting.
My brothers and I stupid
with giddy emotion.

That night I took a mattress off my bed
and laid it on the floor between Atz Lee and me.
We all watched the calf sleep
and took turns to make sure
it was still breathing.
And all night we dreamt
of all the impossible things
we would do when we grew up.

# Sauna

I used to stare up at those cold sharp stars on winter
    nights
stepping naked out onto a cold plank of frozen wood
to escape the heat of the small sauna
which served as our bath every Sunday night.
A turkey thermometer
mounted on one of the four benches
told us how hot it was in there.

We would drink bitter birch sap
mixed with water to cool our insides.
But when the heat became unbearable,
my family and whatever neighbors came
would step outside the door.
Some would roll in snow banks,
some would jump through the thin crust of ice
in the plastic-lined homemade pool that was so cold
it felt like your heart would explode.

Being shy, I'd try and wait to take a sauna until the others
    had finished
and gone inside for thick slices of bread and stew.
Dry heat warming my bones,
mending unknown trespasses.
I would wait until my heart raced with heat and fever
then I would step into the black endless night
letting the cold air rush against my body, steam
rising noiselessly. The mountain ash tree
rustling a few frozen leaves, brittle chimes in the evening
    breeze.

# The Tangled Roots of Willows

I remember as a child
poking at the frozen earth
to expose the roots of willows
encased in glittery sheaths of ice

My father would cut the thin tips
with his pocket knife, wind them
like stiff and knotted rope to carry home

He'd soak them in water for three days
until they were soft
Sometimes using bits of
bone, shell, or feather
as decoration, he taught
us all to weave, many
winter nights spent in
silent concentration

Those were peaceful times,
collecting and unearthing
the tangled roots of willows
in the quiet of night
just my old man and I,
not a thing wrong in the world

# Goodness
## (A Poem for Shane)

My older brother Shane
has always been kind
and would shoulder the lion's share
of our many chores.
Come morning
it was his voice
which would rush my consciousness
into the cold reality of the bedroom we shared.
It was his hands
which would numbly feel for coal
in the still black dawn
to start a fire
and his long fingers
which would grasp the warm pink teats
of the milk cow in the freezing cold
so that I could siphon off the cream
to make butter before school.
He broke up fights between Atz Lee and me
absorbing the kicks and screams
and hollers of rebuttal
without anger.
He was our smiling Buddha
a kind constant force in a house
that was otherwise capricious.

I recently went to the hospital
to see his fourth child,
a girl, being born.
I think I am still a child
scattering myself thin.

But as I watched my brother
with his tiny new baby
and his three boys coming up
to take a peek at their new sister
I thought to myself, he must be
a particular kind of being
a breed of person that is made simply
and perfectly to love.

# Wolves in the Canyon

During snow storms it is always the most quiet.
Sometimes as a child I would leave my bed
to walk out in the white padded dark
and sit at the canyon's edge, tucked neat
amongst the lacy shelter of tangled willows.

The voice of one wolf can spilt itself so that it sounds like
    the voice of three,
so a small pack of wolves sounds like the most lonesome
    chorus.
Sitting out at the canyon's edge,
looking out upon the still strange landscape of winter,
I knew their song.
I felt it deep in my belly.
Sometimes I was sick with it,
so heavy was it in me that all I could do
was open my mouth and let it call out.
It was instantly my comfort.
My own treasure harbored somewhere
behind my lungs, inside my heart.
It was the song of my soul, I imagined,
and I would lend it to the wolves
and sing with them in the still of midnight,
while my brothers lay sleeping,
beneath thick blankets of dreaming.

## God Exists Quietly

God exists quietly.

When I sit still and contemplate
the breeze that moves upon me
I can hear Him.

For hours I would lay
flat upon the meadows
stare at the
endless field of blue sky
and revel in
the divine placement of all things.

I would walk alone
in the woods and let my mind wander
freely, stumble across theories
on the origins of myself
and all things.

In nature I knew all things had
their place. None supreme,
none insignificant and so
great peace would come to me
as I fit neatly in the folds
between dawn and twilight.
Living in sync with the rhythm
of the earth, eating what
we grew, warming
ourselves by the coal fire,

creating
myself in the vast silence that existed
between the wild mountains of Alaska
and our front porch.

I grew to love the
Nature of god.
I knew Him best not in churches, but
   alone with the sun shining on me through the trees

It birthed a space in me
that would continue to
crave the sacred
and demand sanctity
as my life took flight
and lit out to travel
the world.

It has grounded me
and held me steady
in the strong winds
that have carried me
so far from
where I have been.

Prayer is the greatest
swiftest
ship my heart could sail upon.

# Miracle

Listen!

Do you hear it?
I do.
I can *feel* it.
I expect a miracle is coming.
It has set loose this restlessness
inside of me.

Expect it.
Dream about it.
Give birth to it in your being.
Know! Something good
is coming down the line.
Finding its way to you
like all things find their way
to god's children.

Listen!

# Afterword

I had no idea what to expect when *A Night Without Armor* was published. It was my first book, a collection of poetry no less. Up until that point, I had shared my poems with very few people—my mother, Nedra, my friends, my family. But once published, these words were there, in black and white for everyone to see.

I'm grateful, and a little overwhelmed by the response. My publisher tells me the book sold fairly well, but, more important, the poems seemed to touch people. I've received countless letters and E-mail from readers who felt certain poems spoke to them, forced them to ask questions, and helped them through difficult times. I'm glad for that, and for the connections that were formed.

I mentioned in the preface of the original edition that reading poetry was essential to me as a child. It still is today because it taught me about the human emotional process. Poetry is honest. It is not celebrity selling itself with perfect-image marketing: perfectly slim, perfectly happy, perfectly talented. As a child watching television and reading magazines, I felt separate from what seemed to be a race of people who were born extraordinary, with no problems, no hate, no abuse, no hurt. Reading Neruda and Bukowski showed me humans who were good, but also struggling. I could learn from their honesty about their vanity, envy, and self-pity, as well as their hopes for goodness.

As I became a celebrity myself, I began to feel I was part of the "perfect persona" media game, and thus part of the same force that confused me as a child. *A Night Without Armor* was my way of stepping outside of that persona to show myself honestly, as I've developed over the course of time. I thought it was important to include poems from my early years, even if they lacked the technical skill of my later work, because they were true to my confusion, my fear, and dreams relative to my age.

I knew that if I wanted to please critics I would have to put in only my "best" poems. But doing this would have defeated my goal for this book. So I took a risk and put in some material that I would have liked to have read when I was younger. Your support lets me know I made the right decision.

Jewel
JUNE 1999

## Pat Steir

*"Beauty and intellect join forces in Pat Steir's paintings. The pictures may be read as metaphors for the imagination itself, a mercurial space of fluidity and transformation."*

—KEN JOHNSON, *NEW YORK TIMES*,
NOVEMBER 14, 1997

# List of Illustrations

*All paintings courtesy of Pat Steir:*

page ii "Curtain Waterfall," 1991, oil/canvas, 146 x 116

page xvii "Peacock Waterfall," 1990, oil/canvas, 179 x 121

page 25 " Monk Tuyu Meditating Waterfall," 1991, $149\frac{3}{8}$ x $114\frac{5}{8}$

page 45 "The Brussels Group: Starry Night," 1991, oil/canvas, $107\frac{1}{4}$ x $89\frac{1}{4}$

page 64 "Primary Amsterdam Waterfall," 1990, oil/canvas, 59 x 59

page 76 "September Evening Waterfall," 1991, oil/canvas, 289.5 cm x 260.0 cm

page 97 "Blue & Yellow One Stroke Waterfall," 1992, oil/canvas, 174 x $90\frac{3}{4}$

page 122 "Wolf Waterfall," 1990, oil/canvas, 178 x 97

SINGER. SONGWRITER. POET. INSPIRATION.

# JEWEL
## SPIRIT
the multi-platinum follow-up
to her 10-million-selling debut album
PIECES OF YOU
featuring "Hands," "Down So Long" & "Jupiter"